Like a Pro

Cheerleading

Candice Letkeman

AV2
www.openlightbox.com

AV2

Step 1
Go to **www.openlightbox.com**

Step 2
Enter this unique code
AUDEH8V4T

Step 3
Explore your interactive eBook!

AV2 is optimized for use on any device

Your interactive eBook comes with...

Audio
Listen to the entire book read aloud

Videos
Watch informative video clips

Weblinks
Gain additional information for research

Try This!
Complete activities and hands-on experiments

Key Words
Study vocabulary, and complete a matching word activity

Quizzes
Test your knowledge

Slideshows
View images and captions

Share
Share titles within your Learning Management System (LMS) or Library Circulation System

Citation
Create bibliographical references following APA, CMOS, and MLA styles

This title is part of our AV2 digital subscription

1-Year K–5 Subscription
ISBN 978-1-7911-3320-7

Access hundreds of AV2 titles with our digital subscription.
Sign up for a FREE trial at **www.openlightbox.com/trial**

The digital components of this book are guaranteed to stay active for at least five years from the date of publication.

Cheerleading

Contents

I love cheerleading.
I am going to cheerleading practice today.

The first cheerleaders were men. They cheered at American football games.

I wear stretchy clothes when I practice cheerleading. They are easy to move in.

Like a Pro

Cheerleaders wear uniforms for events and competitions.

I bring pom poms to practice. They are sparkly and shiny.

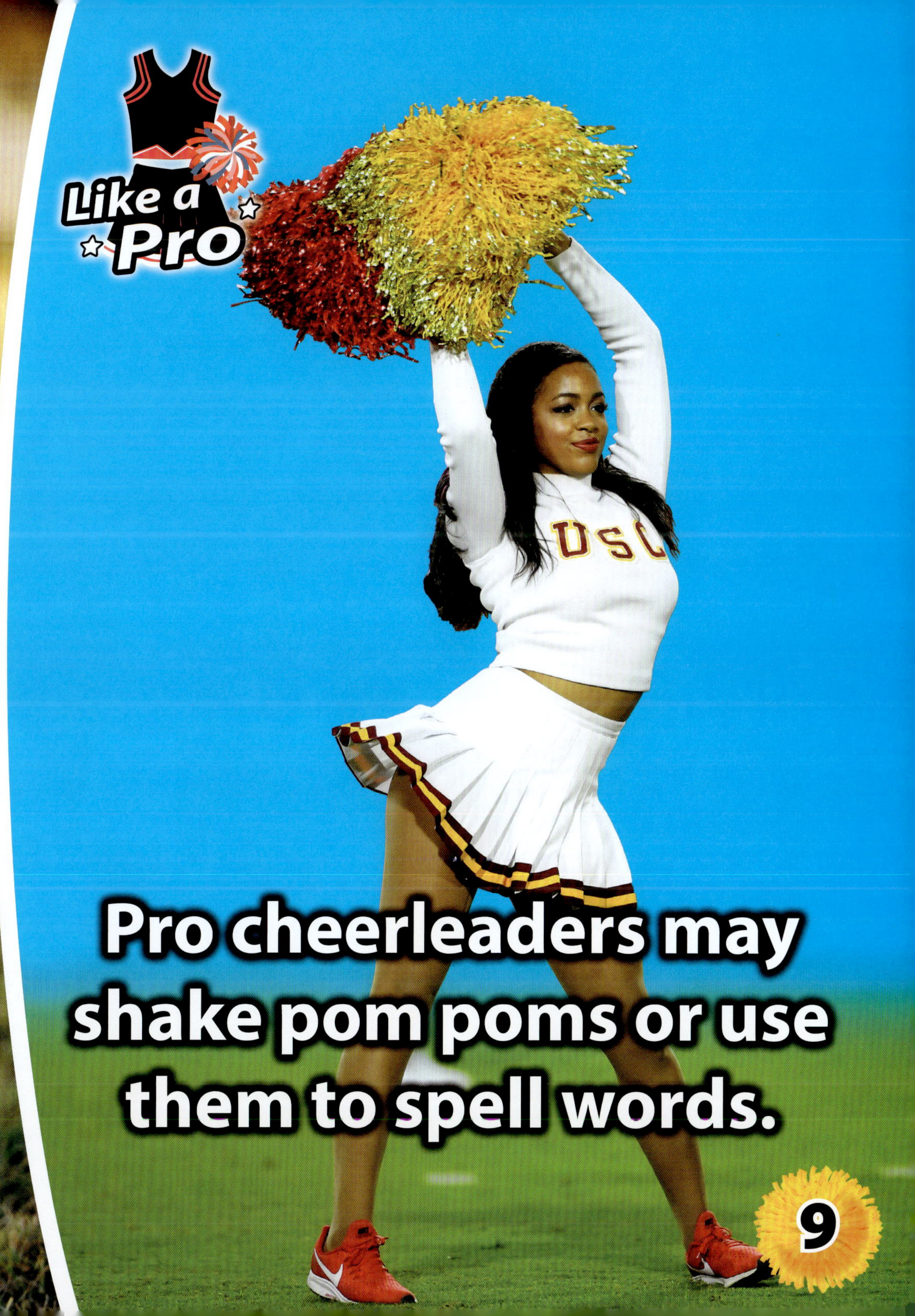

Like a Pro

Pro cheerleaders may shake pom poms or use them to spell words.

I practice cheerleading in a gym. The floor is covered with mats.

Like a Pro

Mats help cheerleaders practice their moves safely.

I warm up before cheerleading.
I run for a few minutes.
Then, I do some stretches.

Like a Pro

Pro cheerleaders may practice for three hours every day.

I meet my squad before a game. We perform our routine together.

Like a Pro

Cheerleading routines may include jumps, tumbles, and stunts.

My squad takes part in competitions. We get points for having high energy and doing stunts well.

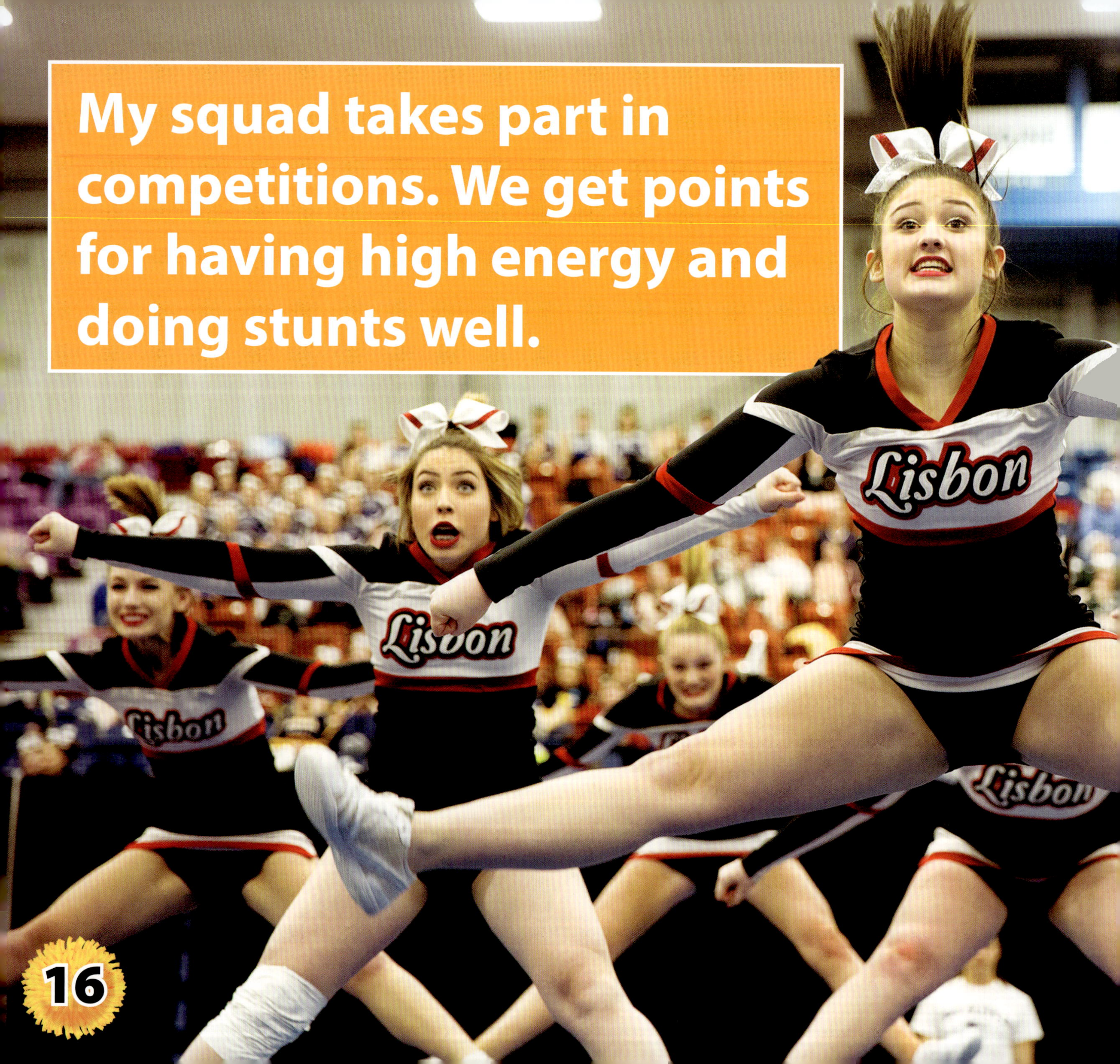

The squad with the most points wins a competition.

Our squad works together. Some moves need more than one person.

Like a Pro

Cheerleaders may work together to make human pyramids.

I love cheerleading.

CHEERLEADING FACTS

These pages provide more detail about interesting facts found in the book. They are intended to be used by adults as a learning support to help young readers round out their knowledge of each sport featured in the *Like a Pro* series.

Pages 4–5

Getting Ready Cheerleading is a team activity that combines elements of dance, acrobatics, and shouted slogans. Cheerleaders entertain spectators at sporting events and encourage them to cheer for the team. Schools, colleges, and professional sport organizations have cheer squads.

Pages 6–7

What I Wear Cheer uniforms consist of a sports top, briefs, socks, and shoes. They are typically in the school or team's colors. The top is a sleeveless shell. A long-sleeved bodysuit is often worn underneath. Female cheerleaders usually wear a short, pleated skirt. Male cheerleaders wear matching tops and pants. Cheer shoes are light, with rubber soles for grip and traction.

Pages 8–9

What I Use Pom poms add style and excitement to a squad's look. They are shiny or glittery to get a crowd's attention. Pom poms have a handle hidden in the middle to make them easy to hold. Cheerleaders shake pom poms to emphasize movement or spell out words. They come in many sizes, colors, and types.

Pages 10–11

Where I Play Cheerleading can be practiced indoors or outdoors. Mats on the floor or ground can provide a springy, cushioned surface. Some competition events are held in school gyms. Others are held in arenas and convention centers all over the country. The largest competition is the Cheerleading Worlds, held annually in Orlando, Florida.

Pages 12–13

Warming Up Cheerleading is physically demanding. Properly warming up helps prevent injuries. A typical warm-up for cheerleaders begins with active stretching and cardiovascular activities. These may include jogging, jumping jacks, skipping, or dancing. Next, every muscle group in the body needs to be stretched to help increase flexibility. Warm-ups last from 8 to 10 minutes.

Pages 14–15

Performing the Routine A competitive cheer routine is about 2.5 minutes long. Cheerleaders usually start with feet apart and fists on hips. When the music starts, they perform a routine. Basic arm positions include the clasp, clap, high V, and punch. Jumps include the spread eagle, toe touch, and tuck. Stunts and tumbling may be performed by pro cheerleaders.

Pages 16–17

Winning the Competition Cheerleading competitions have a panel of judges. They have scorecards with various categories such as stunts, timing, originality, and appearance. Squads are awarded points in each category up to a maximum, which is often 100. Points are deducted for mistakes. After each squad has performed, the one with the most points wins.

Pages 18–19

Teamwork Cheerleading pyramids are a common stunt. They should be no more than two people high. There are three key positions necessary to building a pyramid. The bases are the bottom of the pyramid, and they support the weight of other cheerleaders. The flyers stand on the bases' hands, thighs, or shoulders. The spotter is in place to help catch any flyer who loses their balance or falls.

Pages 20–21

I Love Cheerleading Cheerleaders need to be in excellent physical condition. They keep in good shape by doing cardiovascular and strength-building exercises. Proper nutrition, along with drinking enough water, is important to stay healthy and have energy. Cheerleaders should show respect toward their squad and other squads in competitions.

KEY WORDS

Research has shown that as much as 65 percent of all written material published in English is made up of 300 words. These 300 words cannot be taught using pictures or learned by sounding them out. They must be recognized by sight. This book contains 52 common sight words to help young readers improve their reading fluency and comprehension. This book also teaches young readers several important content words, such as proper nouns. These words are paired with pictures to aid in learning and improve understanding.

Page	Sight Words First Appearance
4	am, I, to
5	a, at, first, like, men, the, they, were
6	are, in, move, when
7	and, for
9	may, or, spell, them, use, words
10	with
11	help, their
12	before, do, few, run, some, then, up
13	day, every, three
14	my, our, together, we
16	get, high, part, takes, well
17	most
18	more, need, one, than, works
19	make

Page	Content Words First Appearance
4	cheerleading
5	American football games
6	stretchy clothes
7	competitions, events, uniforms
8	pom poms
10	floor, gym, mats
12	minutes, stretches
13	hours
14	routine, squad
15	jumps, stunts, tumbles
16	energy, points
18	person
19	human pyramids

Published by Lightbox Learning Inc.
276 5th Avenue, Suite 704 #917
New York, NY 10001
Website: www.openlightbox.com

Library of Congress Control Number: 2023935725

ISBN 978-1-7911-5787-6 (hardcover)
ISBN 978-1-7911-5788-3 (softcover)
ISBN 978-1-7911-5789-0 (multi-user eBook)

042023
100922

Printed in Guangzhou, China
1 2 3 4 5 6 7 8 9 0 27 26 25 24 23

Project Coordinator: John Willis
Designer: Ana María Vidal

Every reasonable effort has been made to trace ownership and to obtain permission to reprint copyright material. The publisher would be pleased to have any errors or omissions brought to its attention so that they may be corrected in subsequent printings.

The publisher acknowledges Alamy, Getty Images, and Shutterstock as its primary image suppliers for this title.